Made especially for

From

Date

FRIENDS
Scrapbook of Memories™

Surprisingly Simple
A LASTING
GIFT of LOVE
PLACE YOUR PHOTO HERE

INTEGRITY®
PUBLISHERS
Nashville

Table of Contents

How to Create Your Scrapbook of Memories™

Congratulations! You have found the perfect gift for your friend! Just add memories and you have a one-of-a-kind keepsake that will be treasured for a lifetime.

As you browse the pages of this scrapbook, think back over precious memories and unforgettable moments. As you fill each page with your thoughts, prayers, and remembrances, you are creating a customized token of friendship that can be shared for years to come.

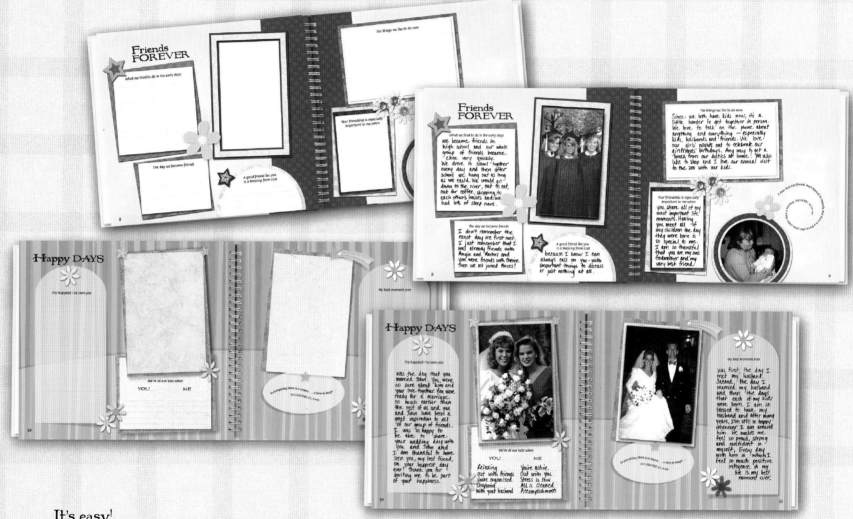

It's easy!

1. Look back over the special times you've had with your friend and record your memories with the help of the prompts provided on each page. (Unsure of some of the details? No problem! Save those prompts as a special opportunity to finish creating the scrapbook with the help of your friend.)

2. Gather favorite photographs and place them in the spaces provided.

3. Write a personal letter to your friend in the space provided.

4. Tear out this page.

5. Save this Scrapbook of Memories for that special occasion and then giggle, cry, and dream along with your friend, as you recall all of the memories you've shared together.

They'll never forget the gift of a Scrapbook of Memories!

Scrapbook of Memories™ Series

A Letter to My Friend

I thank my God every time I remember you.

PHILIPPIANS 1:3 NCV

My Best FRIEND

You are my best friend because

Dear friends, we should love each other.
1 JOHN 4:7 NCV

BEST FRIEND

You have blessed my life by

_____

_____

_____

_____

_____

_____

_____

_____

_____

_____

_____

_____

_____

_____

_____

Friends FOREVER

What we liked to do in the early days

The things we like to do now

The day we became friends

Your friendship is especially
important to me when

A man who has friends must himself be friendly, but there is a
friend who sticks closer than a brother. PROVERBS 18:24 NKJV

A good friend like you
is a blessing from God

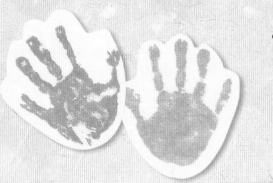

A Small WORLD

You grew up in

_____

_____

_____

Now you live in

_____

_____

_____

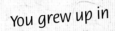

YOU

Name

_____

Birth date

_____

Parents

_____

_____

Siblings

_____

_____

_____

ME

Name

Birth date

Parents

Siblings

I grew up in

Now I live in

Children are a gift from the LORD.
PSALM 127: 3 NLT

What a PAIR!

Our best qualities

YOU   ME

_____

_____

_____

_____

We're passionate about

YOU   ME

_____

_____

_____

We're sentimental about

YOU   ME

_____

_____

_____

A quality of yours I wish I had

_____

_____

_____

_____

A friend loves at all times.
PROVERBS 17:17 NKJV

Our similarities   Our differences

_____   _____
_____   _____
_____   _____
_____   _____
_____   _____
_____   _____

We complement each other in ways

_____
_____
_____
_____

We're talented in

YOU   ME

_____   _____
_____   _____
_____   _____
_____   _____
_____   _____

What I admire about you

_____
_____
_____
_____
_____
_____

Role PLAYS

Whatever you do, do your work heartily, as for the Lord rather than for men. COLOSSIANS 3:23 NASB

You seem to enjoy

The many roles we play

YOU   ME

The role(s) I enjoy the most

Ways I would like to be different

For me, the most difficult role in life

Making MEMORIES

My dearest memory of our friendship

_____
_____
_____
_____
_____
_____
_____
_____
_____
_____
_____
_____
_____
_____
_____
_____
_____

BEST Friends

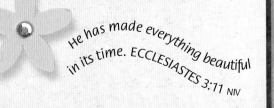

He has made everything beautiful in its time. ECCLESIASTES 3:11 NIV

The best time we've
ever had together

_____
_____
_____
_____
_____
_____
_____
_____
_____
_____
_____
_____
_____
_____
_____
_____
_____
_____

I will never forget the time

_____
_____
_____
_____
_____
_____
_____
_____
_____

Girl TALK

I like to talk with you about

The best girl talk we've ever had

_____
_____
_____
_____
_____
_____
_____
_____

We confide in each other

_____
_____
_____
_____
_____
_____
_____
_____

I go to you for advice on

_____
_____
_____
_____
_____
_____
_____
_____

Swapping SECRETS

You've kept this secret for me

_____

_____

_____

_____

_____

Those who are trustworthy can keep a confidence. PROVERBS 11:13 NLT

Something I've never told you

_____

_____

_____

_____

_____

I prayed for you when

_____

_____

_____

_____

_____

_____

I depend on you for

_____

_____

_____

_____

_____

_____

_____

_____

Just BETWEEN US

"He will yet fill your mouth with laughter and your lips with shouts of joy."

JOB 8:21 NIV

Our special sayings

Our nicknames

YOU   ME

Our inside jokes

_____
_____
_____
_____
_____

Our strengths

YOU	ME

A story that always makes us laugh

_____
_____
_____
_____
_____
_____
_____
_____

Our weaknesses

YOU	ME

Circle of
FRIENDS

Our group of friends

_____

_____

_____

_____

_____

_____

_____

I regret growing apart from

_____

_____

_____

_____

_____

My dear friends, we always have

good reason to thank God for you,

because your faith in God and your love

for each other keep growing all the time.

2 THESSALONIANS 1:3 CEV

I think we enjoy
our group of friends because

A favorite memory
with our group of friends

Just For GRINS

Be joyful always.
1 THESSALONIANS 5:16 NIV

The funniest home-improvement project I've seen you undertake

_____
_____
_____
_____
_____
_____
_____
_____

Our favorite hangout

_____
_____
_____

Events we always meet for

_____
_____
_____
_____
_____

DUTY FREE SHOPPING

For fun, we

_____
_____
_____
_____
_____
_____
_____
_____
_____
_____
_____
_____
_____

On "girls' night out" we

_____
_____
_____
_____

At least once each year, we

_____
_____
_____
_____

HAPPY BIRTHDAY
to Us

How we celebrate birthdays

Greatest birthday celebration we've had

"We had to celebrate this happy day."
LUKE 15:32 NLT

Most meaningful gift you ever gave me

_____

_____

_____

_____

_____

_____

Boring birthdays

_____

_____

_____

_____

_____

_____

_____

Let's CELEBRATE!

Remember when

_____
_____
_____
_____
_____
_____
_____
_____
_____
_____
_____
_____

It was the sound of a great celebration!
PSALM 42:4 NLT

Occasions we celebrate
with our friends

_____
_____
_____
_____

Party disasters

_____
_____
_____
_____
_____
_____
_____
_____
_____
_____

Best party
we've been to

_____
_____
_____
_____
_____

Our FAVORITE Things

YOU	ME
Color	Color
Flower	Flower
Possession	Possession
Sport	Sport
Indoor activity	Indoor activity
Outdoor activity	Outdoor activity
Car	Car
Book	Book
Movie	Movie

YOU	ME
TV program	TV program
Hobby	Hobby
Type of music	Type of music
Song	Song
Quote	Quote
Scripture verse	Scripture verse
Season	Season

33

Bon APPÉTIT

FAVORITES

YOU	ME
Foods	Foods
Cravings	Cravings
Soda	Soda
Coffee	Coffee
Dessert	Dessert
Form of chocolate	Form of chocolate
Ice cream	Ice cream
Snack food	Snack food

Best recipe

"He provides you with plenty of food and fills your hearts with joy." ACTS 14:17 NIV

Favorite way to cheat on a diet

_____

_____

_____

_____

Our favorite restaurants

YOU   ME

_____   _____

_____   _____

_____   _____

What we like to order

YOU   ME

_____   _____

_____   _____

_____   _____

_____   _____

Cherry Pie

Fashion STATEMENTS

Popular trends of our time

Fashion mistakes

YOU	ME
Designer	Designer
Outfits	Outfits
Colors	Colors
Shoes	Shoes
Fragrance	Fragrance
Jewelry	Jewelry
Accessories	Accessories

Strength and honor are her clothing.
PROVERBS 31:25 NKJV

Shop 'til We DROP

And the most important

piece of clothing you must wear is love.

Love is what binds us

all together in perfect harmony.

COLOSSIANS 3:14 NLT

Where we like to shop

Spendy or thrifty?

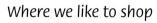

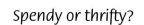

Best bargain stores

Best shopping sprees

Staying FIT (Inside and Out)

YOU

Dieting dilemmas

_____

_____

_____

_____

Best diet

_____

_____

_____

_____

Funniest diet

_____

_____

_____

_____

ME

Dieting dilemmas

_____

_____

_____

_____

Best diet

_____

_____

_____

_____

Funniest diet

_____

_____

_____

_____

<u>YOU</u>　　　　　　　　<u>ME</u>

How we maintain our

Mental fitness　　　　　　Mental fitness

_____　_____

_____　_____

_____　_____

Physical fitness　　　　　　Physical fitness

_____　_____

_____　_____

_____　_____

Spiritual fitness　　　　　　Spiritual fitness

_____　_____

_____　_____

_____　_____

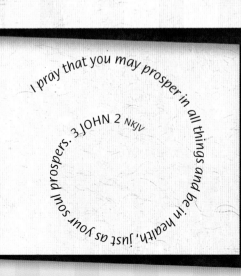

I pray that you may prosper in all things and be in health, just as your soul prospers. 3 JOHN 2 NKJV

41

Beauty
(or the BEAST)

You should be known for the beauty that comes from within, the unfading beauty of a gentle and quiet spirit, which is so precious to God. 1 PETER 3:4 NLT

YOU	ME
Best hairstyles	Best hairstyles
Worst hairstyles	Worst hairstyles

YOU	ME
Makeup	Makeup
Beauty secrets	Beauty secrets
Best looks	Best looks

43

CAREERS

YOU	ME
First job	First job
Worst job	Worst job
Dream job	Dream job

YOU	ME
Education/degrees	Education/degrees
Careers	Careers

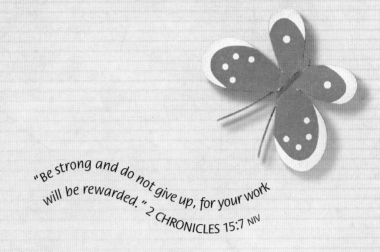

"Be strong and do not give up, for your work will be rewarded." 2 CHRONICLES 15:7 NIV

YOU	ME
Successes	Successes

Away WE GO!

My favorite trip that we took together

_____

_____

_____

_____

_____

_____

_____

_____

_____

_____

_____

_____

_____

Unforgettable moments

YOU

Favorite travel spots

Dream vacations

Worst travel experiences

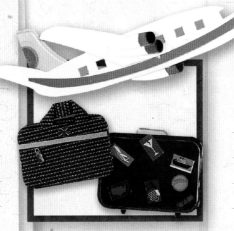

"The LORD your God will be with you wherever you go." JOSHUA 1:9 NIV

TELEPHONE

ME

Favorite travel spots

Dream vacations

Worst travel experiences

Happy HOLIDAYS

"It is more blessed to give than to receive." ACTS 20:35 NLT

Holidays we celebrate together

_____

_____

_____

_____

_____

_____

To me, holidays are a time for

_____

_____

_____

_____

_____

_____

_____

_____

_____

YOU

Simplest gift with
most meaning

_____
_____
_____
_____

ME

Simplest gift with
most meaning

_____
_____
_____
_____

Favorite religious
holiday

_____
_____
_____

Favorite religious
holiday

_____
_____
_____

YOU

Traditions

_____
_____
_____
_____
_____
_____

ME

Traditions

_____
_____
_____
_____
_____
_____

49

Keeping the FAITH

To me, faith is

_____

_____

_____

_____

_____

_____

_____

I knew God was real when

_____

_____

_____

_____

_____

_____

_____

_____

I'm eager to encourage you in your faith, but I also want to be encouraged by yours. ROMANS 1:12 NLT

A turning point in my faith

I thank God for your friendship because

LOVE & Kisses

Funniest experience on a date

YOU

ME

Qualities we like in a man

YOU

ME

Our best double date

Most romantic experience

YOU

ME

Best advice you
ever gave me on love

Happy DAYS

The happiest I've seen you

_____

_____

_____

_____

_____

_____

_____

_____

_____

_____

_____

_____

_____

_____

_____

We're at our best when

YOU _____   ME _____

_____

_____

_____

_____

_____

My best moment ever

_____
_____
_____
_____
_____
_____
_____
_____
_____
_____
_____
_____
_____
_____
_____
_____
_____
_____
_____

To everything there is a season . . . a time to laugh . . .
ECCLESIASTES 3:1, 4 NKJV

Blue DAYS

A time to weep . . . ECCLESIASTES 3:4 NKJV

We helped each other through it by

The saddest experience we've shared

I knew you were praying for me when

_____
_____
_____
_____
_____
_____
_____
_____
_____
_____

When I'm feeling blue, you cheer me up by

_____
_____
_____
_____
_____

What makes us sad

YOU	ME

Crazy DAYS

I'll never forget the day

_____
_____
_____
_____
_____

The craziest thing we've ever done

_____
_____
_____
_____
_____

And a time to dance . . .
ECCLESIASTES 3:4 NKJV

Our most embarrassing moment

We laugh about

Practical jokes

Tough TIMES

Our pet peeves

YOU   **ME**

I can tell you're mad when

Our worst fight

Our most ridiculous disagreement

_____
_____
_____
_____
_____
_____
_____
_____
_____
_____
_____
_____
_____
_____
_____
_____
_____
_____
_____
_____

Dealing with anger

YOU	ME
_____	_____
_____	_____
_____	_____
_____	_____
_____	_____
_____	_____

A time of war, and a time of peace.
ECCLESIASTES 3:8 NKJV

Feats &
DEFEATS

I've seen you be successful

Defeats

YOU

ME

I am proud of you for

_____
_____
_____
_____
_____
_____
_____
_____
_____
_____

Those who trust in the LORD . . .

will not be defeated but will endure forever.

PSALM 125:1 NLT

Real success is

_____
_____
_____
_____
_____
_____
_____
_____
_____
_____
_____
_____

You encourage me by

_____
_____
_____
_____
_____
_____
_____
_____

How the World HAS CHANGED

How the world has changed since we've been friends

The President
today

_____

_____

_____

When we met

_____

_____

Current events this year   Biggest current event when we met

_____   _____

_____   _____

_____   _____

_____   _____

_____   _____

_____   _____

_____   _____

The World
POLITICAL

PASSPORT

United States
of America

Trust in Him at all times.
PSALM 62:8 NKJV

Social issues I am passionate about

When we met   Now

_____   _____

_____   _____

_____   _____

_____   _____

_____   _____

_____   _____

INSPIRATIONS

Qualities we admire in a person

YOU   ME

The most influential people in my life

They have taught me

Whoever walks
with the wise
will become wise.
PROVERBS 13:20 NLT

You make a
difference in the world

Greatest spiritual influence

Amazing PEOPLE

The celebrities that I have met

Women who inspire us

HOLLYWOOD

One celebrity that I would like to meet

Why I would love to meet

The most amazing
person that I've ever met

DIRECTOR

SCENE   TAKE   SOUND

ROLL NO.
PROD.
DIRECTOR
DATE

Making A DIFFERENCE

YOU

Areas of special interest

_____
_____
_____
_____
_____

Where you volunteer your time

_____
_____
_____
_____

Religious groups you're active in

_____
_____
_____
_____

ME

Areas of special interest

_____
_____
_____
_____
_____

Where I volunteer my time

_____
_____
_____
_____

Religious groups I'm active in

_____
_____
_____
_____

Projects we've worked on together

She ... is well known for her good deeds.
I TIMOTHY 5:9-10 NIV

Something I'd like to do with you

Living & LEARNING

"Wisdom belongs to the aged, and understanding to those who have lived many years." JOB 12:12 NLT

You have taught me

The peoples' lives that you've changed

Blessings I ask for you

Something I wish I had done

_____
_____
_____
_____
_____
_____
_____
_____
_____
_____

Lessons we've learned together

_____
_____
_____
_____
_____
_____
_____
_____
_____

Something I wish I'd done differently

_____
_____
_____
_____
_____
_____
_____
_____
_____

Turning POINTS

Some things get better as I grow older

When I was a child, I spoke and thought and reasoned as a child does. But when I grew up, I put away childish things.

I CORINTHIANS 13:11 NLT

Turning points in our lives

YOU

ME

Something I wish I'd known earlier

What's important to me now

What I know now for sure

What Matters MOST

For me, life's biggest mystery

I believe a fulfilled life is

What I value most in life

YOU	ME
Personal mottos	**Personal mottos**
Philosophy on life	**Philosophy on life**
Faith principles that guide you	**Faith principles that guide me**

So these three things continue forever: faith, hope and love. And the greatest of these is love. I CORINTHIANS 13:13 NCV

From
My Heart to
YOURS

My prayer for our friendship

My prayer for you

Our shared dreams

Dear friend, I pray that you may enjoy good health and that all may go well with you. 3 JOHN 2 *NIV*

I will always be here for you because

How I think you'll be remembered

JOLEE'S BOUTIQUE® STICKERS AND JOLEE'S BY YOU™ EMBELLISHMENTS
ARE OFFERED IN HUNDREDS OF INTRICATE STYLES DESIGNED FOR SCRAPBOOKING, CARD MAKING,
AND PAPER CRAFTS. EACH WELL-CRAFTED, DIMENSIONAL ACCENT IS MADE FROM A MIX OF
MATERIALS—FROM PAPERS, WOOD, FIBERS, FABRICS, METALS, FOILS, AND BOTANICALS.
THEY ARE SOLD AT SCRAPBOOK, CRAFT, AND STATIONERY STORES THROUGHOUT THE COUNTRY.